salmonpoetry

*Publishing Irish & International
Poetry Since 1981*

MW01383862

Zecchinos, rickshaws, Gitanes, the Dollywood Express, gunshots, crack, Lorine Niedecker, and the Chasing Rainbows Museum are all woven together in these large-languaged, visioned, spiritual, sensual poems. These poems are smart, energetic, and surprising. They look at America and beyond to universal desires & appetites, all through the microcosm of Dollywood & its rhinestone founder.

SUSAN FIRER

Dolly Parton once said that what she wants to do as a performer is make them laugh a little, make them cry a little, scare the hell out of them and go home. Stephen Roger Powers has taken this to heart and written a book of poems that gives us America through the lens of one of our greatest unnatural resources. Read it and weep, and laugh and cover your eyes. This is Dollywood.

DORIANNE LAUX

The poetry of Stephen Roger Powers has remarkable qualities of provocation and social investigation; its ambivalence is usually comic. Powers combines insight and delight in Americana with a fervent and ancient sense of worship.

JAMES LIDDY

The Follower's Tale

Stephen Roger Powers

Elvis,
I'm glad you're a
Salmon Poet too. See
you in bygena sometime
:)

10th Anniversary Edition

First published in 2009 by
Salmon Poetry
Cliffs of Moher, County Clare, Ireland
This reprint published by Salmon Poetry in 2019
Website: www.salmonpoetry.com
Email: info@salmonpoetry.com

Copyright © Stephen Roger Powers 2009

ISBN 978-1-907056-20-8

All rights reserved. No part of this publication may be reproduced or transmitted in any form or by any means, electronic or mechanical, including photography, recording, or any information storage or retrieval system, without permission in writing from the publisher. The book is sold subject to the condition that it shall not, by way of trade or otherwise, be lent, resold or otherwise circulated without the publisher's prior consent in any form of binding or cover other than that in which it is published and without a similar condition, including this condition, being imposed on the subsequent purchaser.

Cover artwork: Maura Harmon
Cover design & typesetting: Siobhán Hutson
Printed in Ireland by Sprint Print

For Margie, proprietress of Boog's B & B

Acknowledgments

Acknowledgements are due to the editors of the following, in which some of the poems from this collection first appeared:

Blue Earth Review: "Car Horns"
The Broad River Review: "Cleoparton"
Cash Prize Not Included: "Dancing with Christine Made Me Think About This"
Clemson Poetry Review: "And So I Called Him Applebud"
The Comstock Review: "Our Bodies Are Like Blarney Castle and the Eloquence It Keeps"
Copper Nickel: "papa jazz"
Folio: "Bluegrass on Fire on a Dock by the Sea"
Margie: "Dolly Floats"
Migrants & Stowaways: An Anthology of Journeys (Knoxville Writers' Guild): "Only $2 to See the World's Largest Model Railroad Display!"
Muse & Stone: "Talking to the Storm"
Pebble Lake Review: "This Dolly Shirt"
Poetry Midwest: "After Visiting Dollywood Alone"
Poetry Southeast: "Drive My Urn to Dollywood"
Red, White, and Blues: Poets on the Promise of America (U of Iowa P): "Eagles at Dollywood"
Reed: "Woman of My Dreams"
Re)verb: "The Tracks Next to Ray & Ollie's"
Segue: "The Night Before Dolly's Parade" and "After Her Parade"
Shenandoah: "Dolly and the Frog Strangler"
Smartish Pace: "Every Time I Hear Dolly Sing 'The Beautiful Lie'" and "Once When I Left Dollywood Early I Missed a Free Concert Outside Her Museum"
Tiger's Eye: "A Tour from Nashville's Radical Nun"
Touchstone: "The Tracks Next to Ray & Ollie's"
White Pelican Review: "You Can Say for Sure I'm Gone"
Wisconsin Poets' Calendar: "The Night Before Dolly's Parade" and "Niedecker's Poem Was Supposed to Be on the Bar Wall"
Yemassee: "Drive My Urn to Dollywood"

Contents

iv. One of My Old Favorite Songs

v. Grand Marshall Dolly

vi. Milwaukee, Here She Comes

vii. *Dolly's Voice*

viii. *Going Over Home*

*"The road is in my blood. My blood is on the road.
In this we are even."*

J. E. S.

I.

Proem

The Tracks Next to Ray & Ollie's

My wanderlust comes from my father,
who walked in his sleep to meet the trains.

Every night it was the same. My grandmother
heard the bells sewed to his pajamas,
wrung out her all-night-diner towel, and met him
behind the jukebox, where the stairs came down.

A week before her first stroke she told me
how my grandfather once rode the boxcars
after he ran away from the orphanage.
Maybe it was the legend of his own
father that pulled mine, blanket
over his shoulders like a Superman cape,
out of bed and outside to the tracks next door.

Early one dawn my grandmother was busy
dancing by herself to Nat King Cole, nobody
in the restaurant but her and the General,
who sat at the counter mumbling while
he re-arranged the war medals and ribbons
on his coat. She almost didn't catch my father in time.

She found him on the tracks.
He was scooping dirt in his sleep,
sifting it through his fingers, piling it
between the cracked ties in rows of little pyramids.

All that's left of their restaurant now
is one chipped saucer. My father tells me
it got that way after a penny, crushed
by a locomotive's wheel, flew through
the window. This story comes from a man who can't sleep
unless a train passes by in the night. This story
rides with me when I drive north to the lake,
the freight train of my heart opened and unloaded
tonight, rambling freely for once.

II.

Hooray for Dollywood

Only $2 to See the World's Largest Model Railroad Display!

Chattanooga, Tennessee *

Go there. You'll see
little houses, little hills,
little cars, little redbud trees,
little bears, little wash
lines. The little plastic
people look like they'll burst
alive in Halloos and Howdys
and Nice-to-see-yas
and clog dancing.
If you peek really close, down
in the corner, near the end
of the World's Largest Model
Railroad Display, you'll even see a little
person (maybe she's a little
girl and her name is Wanda
Parlapiano) diving into a little
swimming pool, little legs sticking out
of the little glassy fake water
like the ends of broken hairpins.
There I decided on my new
hobby—model Dollywooding.
I will build the World's
Largest Model Dollywood
Display, complete with working
steam train, parking lot,
trash collection service,
bluegrass theater, backporch
ham & beans restaurant with
pie tins, fruit jars, and picnic tables,
lye soap stand, kiddie tree house,

homemade candle store, sausages
frying, little ducks quacking
in spring rain puddles, season
pass photo booth, and maybe
even a tiny little miniature Dolly
Parton on a buggy that putts
through the miniature park
as she waves to all the little fans
that are too small to paint faces on.

[*] **If You Go:**

The Chattanooga Choo Choo
Hotel, remodeled in a long-standing
depot, is an enjoyable side trip.
If you have enough
$$$$ you can spend
the night in a parked passenger
car. If you have only fifty
cents you can ride the rusty
trolley down the rickety
track to the end of the parking
lot and back. But you must pay two
dollars to see the World's
Largest Model Railroad Display
upstairs.

Eagles at Dollywood

They can't live on their own
so they live at Dollywood.
They don't look damaged. They are marble
bookends balanced isolated in black
oaks on the side of the hill
near the country chapel,
their broken wings
healed but too bent to fly.

I count thirteen of them today,
swallow my mountain red
potatoes and onions and Tabasco fried
in a five-foot iron skillet. I stand alone
on the wooden bridge and watch
those watching the eagles—a family
from a Portland suburb, a young couple
from Chattanooga who've just gotten married
at Ruby Falls, a teenager
from Newark with his girlfriend
and his boyfriend, an old woman
by herself from Taipei.

They linger together in the shelter
of the Dollywood shade, they search
their khaki pockets, bluejean pockets,
flannel pockets. A dozen
quarters tumble and tinkle
into the binocular viewfinders
that hide their faces when they look.

But the old Taipei woman doesn't
look. She shuffles away,
opens her mouth
at me, drops her quarter in the
stream where it weaves under the
ripples like a crystal
swinging.

Rides at Dollywood

The Tennessee Tornado loops in wings.
The Tennessee Twister gave me an idea for a story that
turned into an idea for a novel I still haven't finished.
The first time I went to Dollywood I soared on the
    Swing-a-ma-jig,
and the snapshot mom took shows I was a fat, laughing teenager.

Ride the antique carousel before you splash on the
    Smoky Mountain River
Rampage. Dolly's park workers won't let you on the
    wooden horses
if your pants are wet. The Dollywood Express will take
    you five miles
back into the woods, where you'll see some hillbilly
    mannequins on front porches
and black soot from the engine will hang from your eyebrows.

A little log boat winds through Country Fair Falls, and one
    time it got stuck
on a bend until the boat behind us knocked us free. Dolly filmed
a commercial on the Mountain Slidewinder, and she said
    If I'd known
I'd get this soaked I wouldn't have worn my wig. Thunder Road's movie
screen looms like an iceberg, the moonshiner villains cackle
    and crash
in blooming color. Grandpa rocked by himself on Dolly's
    Demolition Derby
because he was too mad at Grandma to go on the Wonder
    Wheel with her.

The Flooded Mine was fun, but you can't go on it now
   because it's closed,
torn down to make room for Daredevil Falls. Remember
   we posed by the waterfall
there, my arm around you, and that picture faded to
   green and yellow
because I left it on the windowsill for too many summers
before I finally threw it away.

Cleoparton

Not all eyes are on Dolly
when ten muscle-bound men in gold
loincloths carry her litter with asp arm

rests through Dollywood. White linen
with a jeweled shawl and ochre stenciled in
diamond bites on her cheek draw card
riffle shutter clicks. A fan of blue

ostrich feathers commands her gleaming men
move faster. Halfway out the exit gate
a boy squeezes in, hand up, and Dolly leans

down, beads in her straight Egyptian
hair swinging, for a quick, careful palm press.

Coat of Many Colors

i.

Twenty-two years ago almost,
we followed the line through Dolly's first Rags
to Riches Museum. There I was,
thirteen years old and in love
like never before. My brother wanted to line up
for another ride. I resisted his impatient
tugs. My nose smudged the display
glass while I studied her father's work boots, her preacher
grandfather's fiddle, her first doll fashioned out of a corn
cob with matchstick-burnt eyes, a replica of her coat
of many colors. I didn't know then it wasn't the original.

I.

For no special occasion at all my step-mother made me a
quilt from my great-grandmother's old dresses. Here's a
piece from the dress my great-grandmother wore when
she found an ancient family tree in her attic with Leif
Ericsson & Eric the Red supposedly faded near the top,
one she wore when she went to the hospital to have her
diabetic leg removed, one from the picture of her on my
dad's Harley, another one from when she was thirsty &
feverish on her hands & knees in the Minnesota fields, one
she wore when she first held me—you can still see the
stain where I burped up on her—one from the day she
died after her corned beef & cabbage last meal at her
favorite Waterfall Restaurant, and there's the one she wore
when she fried potatoes & onions every morning of her
American life.

II.

Today it is raining when we come out of Dolly's
new, expanded Chasing Rainbows museum. Each spangly
drop carries a rolled-up whisper prayer from my
great-grandmother. You can hear
them set loose when all the raindrop
bottles come down on the Dollywood blacktop.

Dollywood Soundtrack

Through the turnstiles, past the Spotlight
Bakery, across from the Old Flames candle shop,
Dolly and the House of Prayer Congregation
country-church sing "Shine On" from the shrubbery.

We take a right to Jukebox Junction. Outside Red's Diner,
strolling singers in poodle skirts and saddle shoes a cappella
"All Summer Long."We stop at the Chasing Rainbows museum.
I stand on the X, face the camera, watch myself
replace Porter Wagoner on the TV for a duet
of "Together Always" with hair-mountain purple-polyester Dolly.

Then it's off to Rivertown Junction and the Backporch Theatre,
where Dolly's Uncle Bill and his shiny red guitar entertain us
with "Swing Low Sweet Chariot" in the Kinfolks Show.
We sit down a minute and clap along.

More recorded Dolly in Craftsman's Valley:
"Hungry Again," "If Only," "In the Sweet By and By,"
plus real mountain pickers and "Rocky Top."

There's no line today, so we shuffle ourselves on the roller
coaster four times in a row until we are dizzy and the strobe in
the tunnel leaves fingerprints inside my eyes.

Outside the Valley Carriage Works, the Mayor of Dollywood snaps
his stretchy green suspenders and hands us ballots
for the Key to Dollywood recipient:

    ____ Dolly the Sheep ____ Salvador Dalí
    ____ Dalai Lama   ____ Dolley Madison

Back at Showstreet bushes boom "Islands
in the Stream."We exit through the Butterfly Emporium,
where Dolly and the Christ Church Choir rafter praise all
leaving with "Put a Little Love in Your Heart."

She'll be happy to know we've taken that advice.

After Visiting Dollywood Alone

I drove up the abandoned logging road in October. My car bounced and rocked in gullies. I took my eyes off the road to watch a fox flick away. I got hung up on a fallen pine blocking me. Gravel snapped when I pumped the gas up and down to get off. I left the car and followed the road through the woods, thought about that time last June early one morning after we drove all night and fog shrouded Laurel Knob. We played hide and seek in the pink and white blooms of mountain laurel bushes until the sun burned away the fog. We called the world below us our game board. Now, at the end of this logging road, I shuffled to a shale outcropping and tiptoed out to the very edge. A red leaf twirled past my face and leaped over the emptiness. I watched it drift and bob in the clear sky, over the mountains that somehow seemed rickety in their solidness, and I wished for fog so that you and I could be phantoms to each other again.

You Can Say for Sure I'm Gone

The whole summer we lived
together she let me drive her 5.0 liter
V-8 Mustang convertible cop
magnet with its GOOD GIRLS
DRIVE BITCHIN TOYS! bumper
sticker that I left on display even
the last time I drove it, which
was Christmas Day last year
when she needed a ride to O'Hare
for a flight to Philadelphia, where
her French boyfriend would meet her
once more (a glutton for punishment?)
and she'd no doubt confess to him
out of guilt that all this time *yet again*
she'd still been stringing along her ex,
who the French guy hated and so did I
(another glutton, the ex was),
and so I hugged her first, promised to put the top up
and hide the keys in the dog
kennel, under the frozen water dish,
convinced myself I didn't care
that she looked back at me before
she was gone through the terminal
doors, and there on the back seat,
with a fat orange inside wrapped in a trace of her
Chanel, was her Santa hat she'd left for me,
shiny new dime in it too,
and I floored the gas, took off from the airport
at 90 miles an hour with that top down, heater
full blast, and I threw out the Dollywood
postcard I'd written her last spring but never mailed,
watched in the mirror as it fluttered
over the tollway in the traffic somewhere
behind me, stamp uncanceled,
wish you were here
crossed out now.

First Page of a Letter from Dollywood to Taipei

(Translated from Chinese by an Unknown, Semi-Competent Translator)

Did you know one of Dollywood's eagles was at the baseball World Series?

Yesterday I did not know what Dollywood was.
There really is such a place.
A wooden wall around the park stands by the road in the woods. I peeked through a crack, saw mini hot rods on a track flashing their headlights, smelled hickory smoke and train coal.

Today I went in. I bought a Dollywood-made glass butterfly. Look at its tints and flushes.

I watched a blacksmith with a long white beard pound molten horseshoes. Listen to his mallet clatter & spark!

I washed my hands with lye soap. I tried on a yellow ruffled dress and a big hat with feathers. An elderly woman with her hair in a bun took my picture. The picture is black and white. I look silly.

Here we can eat pulled barbeque and spit-roasted chicken. Here we can watch carvers emblazon flags on baseball bats. We can ride the Twist & Shout. We can tap our toes to bluegrass pickers.
Dolly Parton music even chirps from speakers in the bushes by the admission gate.

Oh, the glass blowers, instrument makers, and the mountain brook.

I walked among sprinkle notes of dulcimers, pianos, harmonicas, banjos, autoharps, fiddles, mandolins splashing from sassafras like raindrops shaken down.

Want some taffy? And the calliopes, carousels, train whistles at Country Fair and the Village.

Imagine those Smokies creaking to the clouds over this diplomatic garden.

I am now a citizen of Dollywood.

.

III.

From One Lover to Another

Woman of My Dreams

Everyone thinks it's Dolly Parton
who I really think is my fairy

godmother. When I was small I lived
in a yellow house by a lagoon in Monona.
The summer we moved in, lightning

hit the weeping willow in the front yard, sent it
crashing down on top of the neighbor's Buick.
A tornado snuck through not more than a mile
away. In the power outage my father snatched me

still sleeping out of my bed and galloped down
the stairs to the fruit cellar. I woke up with my head
bumping and bopping the railing as he carried me.

The lightning through the basement windows made
me think that's what a love heart
attack in an old man's chest looks like—a million
fluttering lilacs of neon tumbling
and twirling, blood and electricity

with nowhere to go. That's the wet summer
I first noticed the periwinkle
blue glass imbedded in the cement at the bottom
of the front steps. That piece of periwinkle was
about the size and shape of the end
of a french fry. It caught my eye

like you did when I first saw you from the church
choir loft. To think that you don't look anything like
Dolly Parton—to think that even an inch of
standing rain water couldn't hide
that piece of glass—is clear-cut

as backseat highway dozing in the middle of a starry cold night
with your Anne Murray songs low on the radio.

This Dolly Shirt

for Brenda

The only thing she did
when I asked her what city

she wanted to grow old in
was——*Who should I thank*

for faded T-shirts?——was dip
one finger in green paint,

the other in purple, and
draw quarter moons over Dolly's

cracked eyelids quicker
than check marks so I didn't feel

at all her touches touch and go

on my chest. Then came a dollop of red,
two fresh strokes over a worn-out smile——

a little girl's devilish mommy
lipstick mouth.

Forgiveness on All Souls' Day

for Mickey

So she dropped my treasured Dolly
concert camera in my party
beer cup and suds flecked
our costumes and eyebrows
like worn zecchinos flipped off
your thumb. It's not like
I've never taken 7th row center
pictures of Dolly Parton before.

Her Halloween lollipops stuffed one by
one in my shirt pocket made a sweet
enough corsage that I plucked
and ate for days. Last night
I wrote her last letter on cloud
stationery. I turned the paper so the clouds
were upside-down and my words forged
loop-the-loops in their flights to meaning.
If you read between the lines
you'll learn how she quiets the last
few coins rattling around
in this shaken empty
penny bank heart.

Desert Blessing

I see this calliope
hummingbird as nostalgia
for a place we've visited only
once and promise our whole
lives to return to.

Its wings quicken
the year. The blooming
desert around us
will soon dry up
too fast, but the
80-times-a-second
beating of those
wings will never flood
over the dams
of my deaf ears.

The bird, no bigger
than your thumb,
shakes raindrops off the pink
flowers of the ironwood
branches we stand under,
umbrella closed.

I know what
a heart sounds like.
The splashing from
the hummingbird's wings
on your nose and forehead,
it's the only thing
left now I need to hear—
your face, looking up,
sprinkled with this
desert's holy water.

Every Time I Hear Dolly Sing
"The Beautiful Lie"

I think of you,
how we once spent the night on the island
across the lake in Manitowish Waters,
the oars grumbled in the storm
before dawn, the shower scuttled
into my eyes, crept into my clothes
like that morning when we ducked under
the dripping awning at the Rosegarden
Café and the rusty water went in
my collar and down my back.
We rowed past the point and around
the old pines that had fallen in the lake
like broken toothpick teepees. The lantern
on our dock threw a spear
of light through the mist,
an intangible rope, a line of yellow
powder cut by the lightning. We sang
"In the Pines," our first duet, as the sun
came up, skeletal fingers shrouded in sheer
curtains rose above the water,
our voices coaxed the rowboat
to creak against the warped gray wood
as if keeping time with us.
I want someone to stop me again
and say *I have been*
in love with you.

Talking to the Storm

I.

The aging exasperated cats run and hide.
    Only their two tails show from under
the box-pleated bed skirt.
    The storm's chain-link rain
soaks this room with cloud gin.

    The maple saplings in
this neighborhood
    fidget. Little nervous puppies.
I'd rather they swayed majestically
    and curtained away the sky.

Uprooted memories of
    honeysuckle & morning glory
stir through this whole
    hot house like tonic.

My first night in a new place
    always starts with a storm.
The lightning is the lime.

    It's too late now to shut
the windows, so why not
    pour to the rim and forget
        the ice?

II.

The moments after speaking are like the still-warmth of bed sheets
    rising after the pressure of a body has left them.
By now she might be trying to forget

the late summer nights of aged
Mimolette and Alsatian Pinot Gris.
　　　I used to lie close to her so I could breathe

in her Gitanes after she exhaled.
　　　I wanted something that had been in her chest
to also be in mine. They say sound, like smoke,

　　　never truly dies. It echoes forever, growing
quieter until you can no longer hear it,
　　　but it's always still there.

　　　III.

　　　　　Thanks for the drink, kind storm-
tender, but cut me off now.
　　　Put it on my tab.

No, leave the harried and confused cats,
　　　the waterlogged boxes of Dolly
　　　　　Parton albums, the TV you short-circuited.
Let's go for a quick spin.

　　　Blind me all you want to,
rock my convertible with hail and twisters,
　　　make me hydroplane
　　　　　off the road if you feel so inclined.

But take a look at that little house
　　　down the hill there on the corner,
the one with the big balsam
　　　poplar you just toppled.

Woo, that was strong.
　　　Yet there's where it was home.
　　　　　Those glorious full-grown
trees absorbed the bleached hours

of summer, delayed the needlepoint stitches
of eventual good-bye.

My first night in that house
she slept with her leg locked
around mine. She clutched
a fistful of my shirt
because you made her dream
of zombies and a dark-hooded
something/somebody
outside pounding
our bedroom window.

IV.

It's that window
away from the street, the one
with the light still on.

Should I let myself in? I'll only go
as far as *The Singing Butler* in the living room,
I'll only listen carefully for all

our wine words and kiss words
and touch-behind-the-ear words bouncing
back and forth still.

"It's Not You, It's Dolly"

How am I supposed to
measure up to that? she says
after I break and confess how many times
I've seen Dolly Parton in concert. Stupid
me, I don't stop there. I throw in my twice-a-year
journeys to Dollywood, tell her the first is in April
when Dolly arrives in Pigeon Forge to a pope's
welcome, the second is in December when
every inch of Dollywood is knitted with
Christmas lights. She chalks up and sinks
the eight ball on purpose. *And you think*
it looks like a mountain fairy land?
Then she throws her cue on the table.

She fumbles with her shoes
while she's on her way up the stairs.
Across the floor above, her heels
clock a heartbeat, stopped when the
front door latches shut. How quickly she's
forgotten the night before, when we dragged
the mattress downstairs to the pool table and
heaved it on, crossed and uncrossed each
other's legs like sharing two pairs of
chopsticks in the perfect
basement dark.

papa jazz

july afternoon in sultry south
carolina fizzes I buy a rare Dolly
record from papa jazz 700
miles in an airplane just for that
record not to see you

I walk barefoot on the sizzling bridge
over the drainage creek the green
black alien painted on the cement
tells me you are pregnant
a year before you do

under the gazebo I hold my record
close to my chest wait for you
even though you don't know I am there
in the same town in the spongy
smell of swamp grass decaying spanish

moss honeysuckle your body will
bloom with someone else's love
someone else's life
your first drop of milk
will be an unpolished diamond

Our Bodies Are Like Blarney Castle and the Eloquence It Keeps

(The past is kept in a language no one willingly speaks.)

We gave ourselves only to the words shaken off
    our raincoat defenses of stories,
ignored the ancient ones fallen through missing floors
    of banquet rooms,

burrowed in rock walls, hunkered down
deep as dungeons, far under new ones

left on surfaces by vandals' markers and matchsticks.
The note I'd die for you to write with lexemes finally tapped

away at bit by bit, pried out, brushed off, and pinned for display
will say you want me the way the pretty girl

on the platform wants that young man who's just gotten on.
He happens down the aisle bent over loaded bags.

Outside on the platform, she walks along. He doesn't see her
watching him farewell until right before she's gone—

he dive-leans over the newspaper readers in his way,
hallmarks his fingers on the wet, dirty window where she's put hers.

Sometimes when you watch a ceiling fan out of the corner
of your eye, its blades spin the other way, but

of course this train never turns around
the haunted trembling of his lips.

Starlings, startled from the power line along the track,
loop down and up, a foreign sentence across the sky.

Bluegrass on Fire on a Dock by the Sea

for Dolly Parton's banjo

Like the startling fiddler's resin and bows
my horizon is clearly a schedule of barbs—

This is the shore where the
starfish and porpoises wolf all the opposites—

when I hoist you and spin you and ask
you to swim with the dancers and night,

sing me a story that ends with a
dagger of rhinestones and diamond lust.

The fiddles are foxgloves and basses are bollards
and the twinkles of banjos are brighter than moonshine.

Lunar Eclipse Forty Miles from Nowhere

I.

It all comes to this. The rusty black moon above
the horizon is framed in power lines
that skip until we come to a stop on this farm road.
The taillights reflect off a No Passing sign nearby.

Doors left open, Dolly still playing.

After half an hour, a wick of silver, then layers across
the moon—gray, brown crimson, rust black—above this country
road forty miles from anywhere.

The distilled twist of your Angelfire is tart with memory.

II.

In New Orleans I met a homeless man with an infection.

Children dashed between boxcars
to get from the riverside to the Café du Monde.

The river air, the train air, the New Orleans stink air,
the jazz air, the powdered sugar air . . .

. . . I prodded a crawfish carcass
with my toe while I watched him roll
up his pants so I could see his leg, purple squishy on one
side like a Louisiana swamp, rigid swollen white on the other
like packed snow. He wouldn't take my money, just said *Pray*.

III.

One cold morning you and I were on our way to the track.
It was so early the moon and stars were shock-frozen bright, and
a sideshow barker's cloak hung over the whole city
that was waiting to presto reappear. I swung a u-turn
in the middle of the Locust Street bridge, no traffic, and back
the way we came because we were too tired from too many things
to make sure our bodies were happy and fit.

IV.

Rusty black moon with its cake layers of color.

Still, you and I have come to nowhere, and a voice from somewhere
harmonizes from behind the melody Dolly sings,
hums through sharing this cranberry orange cookie with you,
your fingers brushing mine as we both hold it and divide it,

through the dead crawfish, the homeless man with infection,
and now you and me alone in this cool nighttime
under the redressing moon and its feather boa of stars.

IV.

One of My Old Favorite Songs

My Father Still Dreams of Drag Racing

My mother let my father keep
his red Charger for about six

years after their marriage in 1972.
Dolly's *Heartbreaker* 8-track

had a cover prettier than its music—
pink chiffon with her leg hiked up

in puffy peach clouds. I put my hands
together in the back seat.

My father peeled out
of a parking lot. My mother

pressed the ceiling to hold
herself in place.

My father cursed Illinois
drivers on his CB radio. Dolly had

set her wig on disco. "Baby
I'm Burning" chugged through

the seats, shook the windows.
My mother cried when three Illinois
truckers boxed us in.

My mother stayed home.
I went with my father

to a self-service car
wash, my father soaped

up the Charger, I slid coins in
the rinse machine.

The spray gun only dripped. Soap
comets trailed off as we squealed

to another car wash on the other side
of town. I hung my bare feet

out the window and made
believe we were dragging

the sky.

And So I Called Him Applebud

yes, Bud shuttled me to speech
therapy in the afternoon rain.
he spent his days
with little boys who didn't speak
straight, in mini school
busses on clocked time,
with dashboard newspapers and
a yellow bag of peanut M&Ms
peeking out from his green uniform
pocket. his favorite Dolly song
was the one where she picks her
banjo with red-polished nails, sips
moonshine with old Jackson
Taylor in the apple orchard.
his worn-out tape of her greatest
hits hummed and hissed, his cracked
voice barked sideways along—
"But I called him Applejack!"—
because I never told him
I hear you when you talk to me.

V.
Grand Marshall Dolly

Car Horns

I stood around the corner from Rockefeller
Center, waiting for Dolly to come out the side
door, re-playing in my head her Today Show
performance. An old woman with two black garbage
bags over her shoulders, full and bulging as if snouts

were poking from inside, came stooped with no hair,
just a green terry turban like my grandmother
wore for six months after her breasts were pared
off. This barefoot woman hobbled on a hot
sidewalk—sweat dribbled from under her head cover.

Windshields flashed sharper than the sun, gritty
exhaust snarled louder than the musty air from the sewer
grate, fried lamb circled with fish and fountain algae
smells. She did a polka, face cheery, eyes closed, dirty
sweat sparkling like dangling diamond earrings, black
garbage bags jangling and rattling.

One stretched too far and split—
all the aluminum cans inside rolled and clanged
into traffic, bounced off hoods, skipped up windshields,
pinwheeled around roofs and open drivers' windows,
just spun all over everywhere between honks two seconds
before Dolly came out and got in her waiting limo.

A Tour from Nashville's Radical Nun

for Sr. Arlene

I flew to Nashville for Dolly's Opryland
Hotel Millennium Bash. From the airport
Sr. & I prayed through a blind one-lane
tunnel under a railroad overpass
not far from Dolly's mansion.
We found Tootsie's Orchid Lounge & looked
at the pictures from when Dolly stopped in.
I asked if she ever bounced a check
before she became a star. The walls
reiterated the castle-in-the-sky honky
tonk singers who ended up wherever
decades of god-knows-what-happened-
to-him recollections recede.

The woman behind me said,
at the hotel, "Isn't this like church?"
Dolly held open her arms & closed
with "He's Alive." I tried to picture that
stage idol behind the fenced lawn & front
columns of home. Stained-glass window
lights flourished over the ballroom.

Sr. went to sleep in her pink flowerbox
cottage with gunshots next door & crack
practically percolating through
her walls. On Sunday morning Sr.
was the only white woman clapping
& singing in an inner-city gospel
choir, & *The Tennessean* printed
her letter urging acceptance of choice.
I shouldn't have thrown
back the rock wrapped in legal
paper after it smashed her living
room window and scattered shards
like toppled towers of nickels.

Dancing with Christine
Made Me Think About This

I have never put my hand on a pregnant woman's stomach
and felt a baby kicking.

I have seen Dolly's real hair. I have gone to a Dolly memorabilia
convention and told a man grieving with age there why
        I wouldn't join him
in his motel room. I have witnessed riots

    in the name of preserving the hard line, I have heard people
    break themselves on concrete in the name
    of freedom, I have watched them sprinkle their blood
    spirals on the streets of their mother

city. I have almost crashed in an airplane. I have paid
a teenager his father's yearly working salary to fly
me in his homemade glider far over
the Gulf of Riga, I have almost fallen in

    fire—three years old at a campsite in Prairie
    du Chien, belly and bladder bloated
    with warm chocolate milk, and all
    I could think when I stumbled
    in the firepit and mom snatched one
    arm and grandma the other was that the radiant
    logs looked like legs of barbequed chicken.

I have made Dolly recognize me when she sees me
now. She has a special wink and wave
just for me. I have sent a stranger flowers,
I have, drunk and stoned, worn a blue Afro
wig down Bourbon Street, I have put my arm
around Rita Dove and told her she was one
of the most beautiful

women I'd ever seen. I have held a dying friend's
hand, I have received a dying grandmother's
last kiss, I have tried to reunite my brother and his mother
so long estranged they've become a new family
legend. I have loved people I'm not
supposed to.

I have yelled at an entire wedding reception for being nothing
but a bunch of wallflowers. My favorite slow
dance, at that same reception, was with the stranger
I sent flowers to three days later from halfway

    across the country. I have carried a miscarrying
    exchange student into the hospital in the middle
    of the night after speeding down High
    Avenue, I have flown to South

Carolina every three weeks for a year, I have sat
by myself on the home plate of an empty
baseball diamond and cried. I have cried by myself
in a cemetery too, not because I was sad, but
because I was, I thought,

    happy. I have bought my father
    his favorite potato chips for Father's Day
    after his doctor told him he couldn't have
    any, I have listened through the bedroom
    wall to my mother growing stunned at being
    left, I have been caught on a pedal

boat in a thunderstorm, I have felt hail
bruise my head. I have heard a pleasant story
from a stranger lately—

her father taught her to homecoming slow dance in the kitchen
after everyone else finished dinner and the lights had all been
turned off except for a gas lantern on the counter.
   She wondered
if there was a hero lurking in her shadows.

It peeks out of my mind like a snorkeler.
If you've never done it,

   whose stomach
   will you someday place your hand on?

The Night Before Dolly's Parade

I watched an old man watch his son on stage
in *Master Harold*. I ignored the play
and traced his laughs, his lips, his nose, the way
his eyebrows flew up when his son engaged
the audience in something humorous.
After the show I drove all night through states
too flat for companionship. No complaints,
no one to make me feel ridiculous
when I cranked up Dolly's dulcimers down
through Cincy on my way to Dollywood.
I named my future son, sang along, looked
behind while I drove up hills south of town.
My eyes coffeed open to watch for deer
as the rhinestone skyline sank out of my mirror.

Tales from the Tennessee Hills

Would you believe more mail-order sex
toys are sold in the South than anywhere else
in America? A hundred miles southwest of Dollywood,
logging trucks lumber east down Walden Ridge
on Highway 30, the Appalachians in the
distance like an unwound bolt of velvet left unsmoothed.
Saturday night, if he's been paid off, the sheriff looks away
from the snaps of illegal dog fights, and in the morning
an old man in overalls prods with his knobby walking
stick the bloody,
          matted carcasses in the ditch.

The county seat has a small TV station with a call-in
doctor show where the phone lines never light up,
so Dr. Snodgrass reads his paper on the air.
This week the crazy woman in town collects
all the cannabis plants she can find up and down
the mountain, piles them in the back of her pick-up,
and, in an act of protest, lights it all on fire
in front of the courthouse so that the wind blows
the smoke
          through the windows.

The folds in my map are ripped. Sections of Tennessee
buckle and collapse in my lap. Before the dam
I overtake shadows of clouds on the road.
Southern white pines deadened by
beetles have fallen over the train
tracks running along the highway.
I pass a boxy, gilded stagecoach
station that is now Tennessee's most expensive
Bed & Breakfast. By a closed and empty drive-in
at a crossroads near the foothills
of the Smokies,
          a stop sign has faded to gray.

Children vault in hydrant fountains
while a storm flutters on the edge of town.
The band quits setting up because they are afraid
lightning will shoot them into stars.
I have to remind a waiting woman who has one
tooth that it never
            rains on Dolly's parade.

But just about everyone flees in the wrong direction.
The wind grows so strong it blows all the borders
on the maps away and drops them down
in different patterns so nobody knows
what states they've been to. Some of us stay
in the storm, like patient suitcases in the foyer, waiting
for Dolly to arrive at her float
            with its annual fountains & flowers.

Then it's the color of fall dogwood
leaves, her dress and the sky that closes
its taps and opens its curtains
when Dolly appears. She comes out
the back of her van, her wig wide as a collie.
She's all legs and chest, her tulip stalk heels quiver
under her feet, she smiles and sparkles in the setting sun.
A policeman helps her up the ladder to the float,
one hand on her elbow, the other on her leg.
Halfway up, her dress
            pops a button and just about splits.

Of course I've worn my orange and blue
orchid shirt so she can see me, but
the hoot and holler verbal ticker tape
of a thousand wet fans curls around her.
This is always the first sign of spring,

following her float down the parkway
from start to finish—the whole two miles—
without falling down a culvert ditch in the median,
trampling someone's
        blanket, or knocking over a stroller.

A girl in the crowd has brought a Chihuahua
wearing a Dolly outfit. Dolly spots it. She laughs at it.
There are two little red high heels on the dog's hind paws,
a blue dress stuffed with two Hacky Sacks,
and blond pigtails that make the dog
look more like Heidi than Dolly Parton.
I lag
        behind to scratch its ears.

The wind comes down from the mountain again.
Dolly's wig twirls in a tornado
of platinum creepers. All too soon it's all
over, and at the end of the parkway
by the Belz Outlet Mall
they roll her away faster than
your last dime
        dropped under a soda machine.

This is where I'd play a song about whiskey
in my coffee if I had one. This is when
I'm only a detached remora in a burst of blood
zinnias. It's easy to linger here in hope, absorbing
the memory vapors of this place and the moments
leading to now, as if waiting will bring her back
for one more photo op, one more wave,
one more
        dropped rhinestone.

And maybe going home to the roosters squawking
in their own feather-fluttering games,
Chicken Ugly chasing Mrs. Griffin's goat
through the garden, Sneed the sharecropper shooting
the tires and headlights of his rusty Ford,
and our mailman at the stream folding his uniform
neatly on the picnic table before he skinny dips
while doing his route—maybe waiting there will bring back
the night you & I created our own small island where
nothing could break through the love surf
to the humid ghost shores of our bodies glowing
like moons and rising
    above the wobbly bed.

Afterwards I drive alone down the dark parade route.
My windshield is still jeweled with water spots.
The red, white, and blue streamers that have fallen off
the float flicker in my headlights,
mirror my many
      missing faces back at me.

Dolly Floats

1999

Dolly waved from the top of a shaving cream
mountain with a ruby & yellow stained-
glass window pressed into it.
At Dollywood I listened to her gospel
concert in her Celebrity Theater.
We heard her sing High
and Mighty, The Seeker, and
I'll Fly Away.

2000

Dolly sat among asters and vines on a high
park bench with butterfly wings
flapping on the back. This is the year
Dollywood opened Dreamland Forest.
Dolly high-heel-skipped out on stage
in a white fairy outfit with a sparkle wand.

2001

Dolly throned on a globe big as
The Biggest Ball of Twine on Highway 80.
Her red & blue glittery dress with stars rippled.
That dress now hangs in her Chasing Rainbows
museum in the Dolly's Closet exhibit.

2002

The Wright brothers attached a glider
to a tractor. Dolly zipped up her army jacket,
swung her goggles, showed off her tight green pants.
This is the year I missed
the free surprise "Thank You" Dolly Parton
concerts. I hear she wore a denim
mini-skirt & vest, and long-nail-picked
her banjo like you've never heard before.

2003

A fountain float.
In an Asian red gown with a high slit
Dolly crossed her legs and dangled
her black shoe from her toe.
The next day they pulled her too fast
through Dollywood in a rickshaw too low
for most of the crowds to see her.

After Her Parade

The lights are off, everybody's gone
home. Dolly walks alone through Dollywood.
She listens to her heels tap like whatever

raps lightly on my bedroom door.
The wooden gristmill wheel creaks, lumbers
round and round. She stops,

feels on her fingertips
the electricity in an eagle's fallen
feather, smells the dead fires

that have cooked glass, potatoes,
sausages, and horseshoes all day.

She enters her new Chasing
Rainbows museum, steps down

the grand staircase, one hand
on the railing, one hand
over her heart. Her old dresses hang

empty on display, video screens
toss shadows, a wall of magazine
covers grins back at her.

She closes her eyes, dreams of her
coat of many colors gliding
arms outstretched in the wind over autumn
leaves and wildflowers,

sings a few lines of "Wayfaring
Stranger" loud enough so she echoes
and the sequins and rhinestones on

all the dresses
jingle like the bead curtain
over my entryway back home.

VI.
Milwaukee,
Here She Comes

Remember How Storms Seemed to Last Longer When You Were a Child?

Dolly thinks a lot
of her fans are
weirdos, but please
  Oprah, I need a Harpo
  Hook Up to help me
  pull a few strings.
I've met James
  Dickey's mistress,
  Brooke Shields,
  Weird Al Yankovic,
  Little Jimmy Dickens,
  Lucille Clifton
  (after too much
  gin and tonic—
  not her, me),
    Cooter from the
    Dukes of Hazzard,
    even her sister Rachel,
plus some famous poets
who've scoffed at my Dolly
poems, like Carla
Harryman, Claudia
  Rankine, and Charles
  Bernstein, who said I should
  put my non-Dolly words in
  a purse, jumble them up, and
  pull them out one by one
  to write a poem (Cornelius
  Eady only had good things
  to say—he called her
  pure Americana),

but I've never told
Dolly how Dollywood
gives me the best
 food for my money
 at a theme park, that
  I've survived two accidents
  while going to see her there,
   that building another Dolly-
   wood in Japan is a silly
   idea, that I really
   want to be in a
   Dollywood commercial.
And Oprah (I'll ask
Dolly this too)
 have you ever noticed
  the exact moment when
  the dawn comes,[1] or
   when everyone you know
   entered your life?
   Have you ever,
   in your doze dreams,
    recalled places you've
    never been to? [2]

[1] Dolly's sung 9 to 5 so often, does she hear it first thing when she wakes up & gets ready to display herself?

[2] My favorite part of a Dolly concert is when the spotlight snaps on and she steps into it all aglow, sparkling, smiling, ready to pick her rhinestone butterfly banjo until it smokes.

Dolly at Club Tres Hermanos

Another One for Mickey

Dolly comes through
the kitchen door after
Mick and me finish our house
margaritas on the rocks. Second round
already. Mine are doubles 'cause
I'm a big tipper.
Dolly picks a pink lily
blooming from my shirt.
No, she picks two, one for
behind her ear, the other
for my empty margarita
glass. Her red fingernail
traces a shamrock
on Mick's green sweater.
It looks like a cookie
cut from dough, this shamrock
Dolly peels from Mick's green
sweater. Dolly knows
I love Mick more
than her, so away
through the kitchen door
Dolly goes,
heels tocking under the mariachi
band. Mick and me order
one more round.
Just one more
before we go home.

Dolly at the Bat

Strike one, she breaks a nail.
The crowd boos
the pitcher.
She tugs on her pink leather pants,
brushes a strand of platinum hair
from her eye, re-adjusts
her rhinestone-decorated Brewers cap.
Strike two, she pops a button.
The crowd roars
for a relief pitcher.
Her designer hops
from the dugout to pick the button
up from the dirt
and sew it back on.
He also touches up her mascara.
They call a time-out for all this.
A Dollywood commercial plays
on the scoreboard.
She taps her bat on the plate.
She spits tobacco juice.
(She's from the hills of Tennessee,
she knows how to do that.)
The pitcher winds up.
She squints, bites her lower lip, swings.
And wouldn't you know it, this time she rips
the cover off the ball. When the dust clears
she's kissing Bob Uecker
while her designer runs the bases.
It would be impossible for her in those heels.
And the people are happy, the hot dogs
are fresh, the beer keeps flowing through
the seventh inning stretch.
Nope. I told you, this mighty icon never strikes out.

Dolly Rehearses for a Surprise Appearance with the Hillside Ramblers

What a place
Lucky's will be when Dolly
shows up. That's why tonight
the three-guys-and-a-girl band
plunks away with her
in Paula's living room.
Paula's son Frank is the banjo
player, a cool high
school junior with wild
hair and a taste for string
cheese and Jimi Hendrix t-shirts.
He's never seen a woman like Dolly,
but he politely keeps his eyes
on the fret board and bobs
his head in time. The three
other players are his friends,
so taken by bluegrass they
haven't been aware of the tight
shaken bottles of adolescence.
Until maybe now.
Dolly whittles off notes high
and sharp as sinful crystal.
The banjo tings, the bass
goes oomp ump oomp ump,
the mandolin rings and bubbles,
the guitar shicks and hums.
This is what a lonesome silver
necklace sounds like if we hear it
fall in the moonlight stream
and roll away over rocks
in the water glinting.
But time is kind
to this: wine, old friends,
sons and music,
a legend that never ages.

Emerald Hot at Elliot's Bistro

for Diana

An additional woman crosses her legs in the mural
where customarily only one has tea
in the company of roses and a black purse
on the white tablecloth.

The new woman's hair is brimful
as the usual one's cartwheel hat, dress just as tight,
lips as red. But both women's lips are moving,
thinks Chef Pierre from Normandy, although he's not sure
there ever was only one. It's hard to mark shifts
in art after it's settled in the corner of your eye
each day flambéing at table sides.

Pierre points her out to the bonita martini-shaking bar manager.
She's not sure either, and says the extra woman maybe looks
like the singer her professor plays. If they were closer they'd hear
them conversing about Trocadero the Eve of St. Sylvester
and the one's trek through Place Pigalle after midnight in search
of the only twenty-four-hour pharmacy in her
    arrondissement, where
whiskered bums came leering and tapping
on her taxi window out front of the cabarets.

What happens next happens fast,
faster than what runs through a deaf boy's mind
in a confessional when he can't understand what the priest says
after *forgive me father for I have sinned* because there's
a screen and the deaf kid must read lips.

He doesn't know his sins so he confesses in panic,
as quick as he can make them up,
the sins he imagines he'll commit some night
when a singer steps out of a mural to a bluesed-up Storyville
jazz ensemble led by a soul-growling saxophonist—
"all I learned was how to get to heaven," the singer sings,
"but let me tell you it was hell"—and she winds her way through
the halted clatter of the dining room, touching old men's chins,
until the clover fringe on her dress swings out the door,
a shadow hands her a pink tasseled umbrella, and then
she's past a lucky penny and in a white limousine
parked two doors down before the Pinot swirlers recognize
who she was.

Dolly Watches *Brokeback Mountain* at the Oriental

Against Rev. Albert Mohler

Here in this landmark theatre, one of the ten
best in America according to *Entertainment
Weekly*, you'd miss Dolly
sitting in the far back corner alone.
She blends in here so well it's like she wears
the Kimball Theatre Pipe Organ, the chandeliers,
murals, draperies, lions and elephants,
the oversize Buddha statues, the minaret towers.
And who's to say she wouldn't?
"If you can accept me, I can accept you,"
she quipped in *USA Today* about the song
she wrote for *Transamerica*.
She says it's all right to be
who you are, and so
even Dolly Parton receives hate
mail and death threats.
These death threats don't much concern
internet bloggers or Reverend Mohler.
Clever man, in response
to Parton he quoted the Apostle Paul
in Galatians 1: 6-10 instead, because sex
and acceptance are obviously more
important to decry than threats against human life.
"I've always been a weird, out-there freak myself,"
Dolly also said, perhaps in explanation as to why
she seems to accept this Reverend Mohler too.
And five seats to her left is a fan who's noticed her
but leaves her in peace. He's not paying much
attention to the film. He misses the days
when you could look up and see cigarette
smokedust blue dancing in the projector beam.

Arlen Takes Her on His Harley-Davidson

For Noreen, Marlo, and Ryan

I'm the Guy with the Horns,
Texas longhorns on my helmet six feet wide.

Soon as I adjust these green eyeball
goggles——like them?——you put on a helmet

else your wig will fly off.
I'd turn around for it, of course,

spear it off the road with a horn tip,
but don't want you to hurt your pretty

little head. Ride sidesaddle if you like, I'll show you
the Mitchell Park Domes first——you'll catch a whiff of

yeast and hops from Miller Brewery over there.
The locals say the domes are you

with an extra one growing from the ground,
hope you're not offended but that's how it is.

When we get to Lincoln Memorial Drive
cars will start tooting so you might want to wave,

but use one hand to hold my jacket right here. Tight,
tight as you can.

On Brady Street, in front of the Nomad or Rochambo,
a *Journal Sentinel* photographer will wait for us,

maybe the same one who took pictures
of you for Summerfest years ago.

Crocker Stephenson might ask you a question, "Are they real?
Has Kenny seen them?" Okay, two questions.

Down Water Street, JD from the Comedy Café
has to stop alongside on his own Harley,

probably bigger than mine. He'll nod, lift his shades,
our bikes will rumble like two strange dogs.

"Nice catch," JD will no doubt say, and he'll roar off
to Pitch's before you can blow him a kiss.

County Clare is where you'll see the hidden Milwaukee,
and that's where I'll take you last, case you like bangers

and shepherd's pie, stuff like that.
Might see Dennis Getto writing at the bar with a paper bag

over his head—bet his blush will bleed through it
if you rub his thigh and ask him what's cooking—Susan Firer

in her evening gloves of lilacs and gown of peonies,
James Liddy, red faced by the peat fire,

talking of the Waterfords,
drinking a Smithwick's, reading a poem

while you fix your helmet wig—I'm sorry
but you really got to wear one—

and, yeah, "It's futile,"
Liddy will suppose like the poet he is,

"to try revisiting every place
you've been before you die."

Niedecker's Poem Was Supposed to Be on the Bar Wall

(But We Found It in the Closet!)

If Dolly Parton knew Wisconsin
wanted to tear down Club 26
to make room for a 4-lane,
she'd buy all the blue-rimmed
martini glasses, the wooden fish,
the circular bar, even
the bartender if she thought
he was cute enough, and
she'd ship it all down to
Dollywood on an oversize load
flatbed truck, set it right
between the Dreamland Forest
Treehouse and Daredevil Falls
so that all the hot people
visiting the hills of east
Tennessee can enjoy Niedecker's
favorite grasshoppers on a southern
July afternoon.

Dolly and the Frog Strangler

I was writing a song with Dolly when we ran out of gas
near exit 201 going south through a sudden downpour in Indiana.
The first verse was something about how hay bales grow
darker in the rain and the sides of barns turn from red to brown.

We were also hauling a Dolly Parton pinball machine by Bally.
The backglass was in the backseat. The playfield, with rubber
flippers intact, cartoon Dolly barefoot in denim shorts,
    was too big to go
in the trunk all the way. It hung over the bumper by bungee
    cords. Every bump,
my worn-out shocks groaned and banged like rickety
    roller coasters.

We waited for a trucker to bring us a gallon. Hail popped
    on the roof
like too many warped records playing at the same time.
    We were bored,
looking for ways to amuse ourselves. Dolly tapped her
    dragon lady nails
on the dashboard. I used my sleeve to wipe away
    windshield fog.

After we hummed a middle C we wrote the second verse,
something about long hair between your lips and mountain
    berry shampoo
scent in your nose when you kiss someone in the wind.

We rolled down the windows to let the storm heat evaporate
some of the air conditioning. Dolly's wig got tangled and wet.
The strangest thing was happening: The pinball machine
kept flashing hot pink and lavender.

Maybe lightning hit the cord trailing behind. Or else
    something lit it
up from our mind's eye that saw corn tassels rolling in
    this gully washer
over the fields as applauding hands of cheering crowds.

Our chorus was something about how you look out
your rearview mirror and it's still visible after a mile
passes, maybe two if the countryside is flat, but then it fades
away and is gone, and you can't remember anymore what mile
marker it was by when you passed it.

VII.
Dolly's Voice

Don't Ask, 'Cause I'm Not Tellin'

What woman wouldn't be
pleased when a man buys her
cookbook so he can
try some of her famous
recipes at home,

isn't surprised when he knows
the names of all her brothers
and sisters, and can rattle them
off faster than she can,

isn't flattered when
he drives cross country
to Dollywood every April?

At the same time,
what woman wouldn't
worry about that?

Now, honey,
you can write all the poems
about me you want, because some
do move me to tears,

but I'm still not telling you the secret
ingredient in my chicken and dumplings.

I'll Be Back in Nashville by the Time You Fall Asleep

I'll fluff my wig on
its styrofoam head,
unlock my real
curls, rub
off some eye
shadow, pull the belt
of my fleece lavender
robe tighter, say
to my husband
You should have
seen that guy's
loud Hawaiian
shirt this year!

VIII.
Going Over Home

Once When I Left Dollywood Early I Missed a Free Concert Outside Her Museum

When Dolly reads this book I hope she hangs
my picture crooked over dresses bought
for shows I wasn't old enough to see.
The first of many times I went to Dollywood
I didn't wave to her because she left.
Her bus just up and rumbled off before
I knew she stood exactly where I set
my heart on seeing her. My father said
Oh, shit. And then there was the time
fatigue from travel drove me home and roads
of night unrolled for miles. I stopped at the wayside
at the end of the Trail of Tears and rusty wire
around my ankle pulled me under crunchy leaves.
This logging road is where your specter trails
still linger. Ride with me until your lips,
like apple peelings, curl away from words
on pages. All who've driven by in the dark
now pass through me like nets of sparrows.
The places they've been to drop dust
sequins into my eyes.

A Place for the Genuine

I, too, dislike it.
    Marianne Moore

My fourth of July flag is tattered. It has had
enough of two-hour lines for two-minute
rides, hillbilly mannequins
on restored porches, velcro costumes in old-time
yesteryear pictures, eagles in amphitheaters, Pigeon
Forge heart attack traffic, arcades
in the foothills, bluejean outlet stores, $30
bungee jumping, popcorn, peanuts, cotton

candy, corn

dogs. Ouch. The stripes have unraveled
so they flap independently like cash
register tapes in my tree. Sometimes I go

to Dollywood just so I can drive
home through the mountains at night.

The Watts Barr dam is my runway high
over the Tennessee River. The tires click,
the sunroof croons with cool night
spring air. The curve in the middle

of the east tower of the TVA
nuclear power plant is Dolly's waist,
the steam is her wig, the blinking red
lights are her sequins and rhinestones.

Drive My Urn to Dollywood

in the backseat of Aunt Lu's ice cream
white 1975 Lincoln Continental. Drive slow,
follow the scenic Kentucky byway through Mud
Lick, pass the grassy old drive-in theater just before
the Tennessee state line, roll through Livingston
and crooked Overton County,
where I sat one July afternoon in a crowded second

floor courtroom with broken air
conditioning. A fat sweaty judge
said *Land Sakes Alive* and dismissed me
after twenty minutes.

Go the Wears Valley route,
beat traffic the back way into Pigeon Forge.
Stop in Sevierville, take a picture of my urn balanced
on the head of the bronze Dolly Parton statue. Powder her nose

with some of my ashes. Say a prayer for me,
thank that air conditioner for breaking
down. Continue to Dollywood, wait in line for the Tennessee
Tornado, scribble a haiku in my memory,

then sit in the very last row of the roller
coaster, hold the cover of my urn tight until you corkscrew
through the last butterfly loop. When you're upside
down at the top let my ashes fly.

STEPHEN ROGER POWERS was born in Madison, Wisconsin, and grew up in the cornfields of nearby Sun Prairie. While working on his PhD in English he wrote a stand-up act about his hearing impairment and performed for several years in comedy clubs and casinos around the American Midwest. Today he splits his time between Milwaukee and Georgia, where he teaches at Gordon College and enjoys the beaches of Tybee Island. *The Follower's Tale* is his first book. He is also the author of *Hello, Stephen* (Salmon, 2014).

**The Salmon
Bookshop**
& Literary Centre

Ennistymon,
County Clare,
Ireland

www.**salmon**poetry.com

"Like the sea-run Steelhead salmon that thrashes upstream to its spawning ground, then instead of dying, returns to the sea – Salmon Poetry Press brings precious cargo to both Ireland and America in the poetry it publishes, then carries that select work to its readership against incalculable odds."
TESS GALLAGHER